Harvest Time

Contents

R *Indicates page is reproducible.*

Teacher's Guide

Teacher's Guide at a Glance

SUMMARY

Harvest Time introduces students to the importance of the harvest and ways we celebrate its bounty. It describes how geography and climate affect crops. The book extends students' knowledge of how people in different U.S. regions work hard and then enjoy the fruits of their labors.

The Big Book *America's Regions* provides important background information that can be used to support and enrich students' understanding of regions.

In addition, the Big Books *Getting Information from Maps* and *Charts, Graphs, and Diagrams* provide opportunities for instruction in key social studies skills.

MAIN TEXT STRUCTURES

➤ Description
➤ Compare-and-Contrast

SOCIAL STUDIES BENCHMARKS

➤ Knows economic activities that use natural resources in the local region, state, and nation (*Economics*)
➤ Knows how communities benefit from the natural environment (farming on fertile land; harvesting seafood) (*Geography*)
➤ Knows how the characteristics of places are shaped by physical and human processes (*Geography*)

READING BENCHMARKS

➤ Uses the various parts of a book (table of contents, glossary, index) to locate information
➤ Uses text organizers (chapter titles, headings, typeface, graphic features, captions) to locate information and predict content
➤ Connects text with prior knowledge
➤ Identifies structural patterns or organization in texts (description, compare-and-contrast)
➤ Summarizes, interprets, and synthesizes information
➤ Uses simple strategies to determine meaning and increase vocabulary for reading

WRITING BENCHMARKS

➤ Brainstorms ideas, takes notes, and uses graphic organizers to organize information (prewriting)
➤ Creates paragraphs that follow an organizational pattern, uses details to support key ideas, and shows variety in word choice and sentence structure (drafting and revising)
➤ Corrects spelling, punctuation, grammar, and mechanics (editing, proofreading, and publishing)
➤ Writes a compare-and-contrast paragraph
➤ Follows guidelines to evaluate own and others' writing

CONTENT VOCABULARY

The root form of each word that appears in boldface type in *Harvest Time*, along with its definition, can be found in the Glossary.

TEACHING NOTES (TG PAGES 4–9)

The questions and activities in this section provide students with opportunities to practice specific nonfiction reading skills and other important strategies to achieve reading fluency and comprehension.

Before Reading

The **Before Reading** section provides questions that connect students' experiences and background knowledge to what they will be reading. It also provides a graphic organizer that students will use and add to as they read (TG page 8). The organizer will help them to maintain continuity throughout the book and to summarize what they have learned when they have completed their reading.

Reading the Book

The **Reading the Book** section guides students through the book, chapter by chapter. It includes the following:

➤ **Content Objective:** a summary of the chapter's "big idea"
➤ **Discuss the Chapter:** open-ended questions that serve as springboards for continuing discussion of the book
➤ **Information Literacy:** questions to develop students' skills in using nonfiction features such as maps, sidebars, diagrams, and graphs to help make meaning from the text
➤ **Vocabulary:** suggested ways to help students get the meanings of unfamiliar words
➤ **Graphic Organizers:** a variety of ways to help students organize and synthesize the information they have read in a chapter. One of these appears as a reproducible page (TG page 9).
➤ **Comprehension Check:** summarizing questions that activate thinking on three different levels, from recalling facts to analyzing and synthesizing information. This **differentiated instruction** allows *all* students to see themselves as successful readers.

After Reading

The **After Reading** section provides a summarizing activity and gives students the opportunity to share their personal responses to the book.

WRITING WORKSHOP (TG PAGES 10–13)

The **Writing Workshop** provides step-by-step instructions for guiding students through the writing process, using paragraphs in the text as models for writing one or two paragraphs of their own.

➤ Students analyze the **model paragraphs** to identify what makes them good examples of a specific type of paragraph (cause-and-effect, problem/solution, descriptive, informative, etc.).
➤ Students go through the stages of the **writing process** to create similar paragraphs of their own.
➤ At the **revision** stage, students concentrate on improving their paragraphs with respect to one particular **target skill.** Students practice the target skill by revising one or two sample paragraphs on a transparency they can work on together. (Use reproducible page 12 of this Guide to make a transparency.) Then they apply the target skill to their own paragraphs.

➤ After they have revised their paragraphs, students use the **Writer's Checklist** (TG page 13) to evaluate their own writing in the Student Evaluation column. The checklist provides a column for Teacher Evaluation as well and can be used at a later time as the basis for a teacher-student conference.

ASSESSMENT (TG PAGES 14–16)

Opportunities for ongoing **informal assessment** are included throughout the Teaching Notes in the following ways:

➤ Open-ended critical thinking questions in the Teaching Notes allow you to observe students' thought processes and assess comprehension.
➤ Information Literacy features assess students' ability to make meaning from various types of informational texts.
➤ Thinkaloud demonstrations assess students' ability to figure out meanings of unfamiliar words through context clues, structural analysis, and the use of the Glossary.
➤ Comprehension Checks at the end of every chapter provide an opportunity for differentiated assessment of students' content comprehension. These questions require oral reading from text to confirm both written and oral responses.
➤ Summarizing activities in the After Reading section let you assess students' ability to grasp and synthesize key ideas.

Opportunities for **formal assessment** include:

➤ The ongoing reproducible graphic organizer on page 8 assesses students' ability to relate information and concepts from different sources and provides an opportunity for portfolio assessment.
➤ The Test Your Knowledge blackline master on page 14 assesses students' content comprehension and success in meeting both the social studies and reading benchmarks. Answers are found on the inside front cover of this Guide.
➤ The Performance Assessment blackline master on page 15 and the Scoring Guide on page 16 help you assess students' abilities to apply their learning and synthesize information.
➤ Writing activities in the Writing Workshop allow you to assess students' ability to write meaningful, well-organized informational text.

Before Reading

Explain to the class that all readers bring their own knowledge and experience to a book. Point out that connecting what they already know to what they read can help them better understand the new text. Have students apply their prior knowledge to *Harvest Time* by answering the following questions:

➤ What is a "harvest"? Use the picture on the book's cover to help you answer the question.

➤ What crop(s) grow(s) in our area? If you have been apple, pumpkin, or berry picking, describe the experience.

➤ What harvests do you think you might read about in this book?

Tell students that they can fill in the following **Harvest Festival Facts** chart as they read about harvest festivals in communities across America. Some information is already filled in to help students get started.

Harvest Festival Facts						
Crop	**Location**	**Festival Month**	**Climate/ Soil**	**Events**	**First Festival Year**	**Other Interesting Facts**
	Ohio					
Straw- berries					1983	
				Potato sack fashion show		
			Warm, long grow- ing season, lots of rain, flooded fields			Attracts about ten times the town's population
	Maryland					
Choke- cherries						

Reproducible page 8

Reading the Book

Tell students that good readers like to discuss and share ideas about what they read. Let them know they will be discussing the important concepts in each chapter. Then they will go back into the text to answer questions about what they learned.

FESTIVALS AT HARVEST TIME   PAGES 2–5

Content Objective Students will discover that people across America celebrate their communities' harvests with festivals. They will learn that the crops grown in each region are determined by climate and geography.

Vocabulary: Using Context Clues

Have students locate the word *Precipitation* in the map heading on page 4. Explain that readers often figure out the meaning of words by looking for clues in pictures and in surrounding words and phrases. Have students read the map caption. Model for the class how to figure out a word's meaning by using context clues.

> To figure out the meaning of *precipitation*, I will look for clues in the other words on this page. The map caption reads: *Can you tell how much rain, snow, and other* **precipitation** *falls on your state in a year?* If precipitation falls, and rain and snow are two kinds of precipitation, then I guess it's anything wet that falls from the sky—including sleet and hail. I look at the Map Key, which reads: *Annual Precipitation in Inches.* Rain and snow can be measured in inches, so I'm probably right. I'll check the Glossary.

Information Literacy: Reading a Map

Why are there two maps of the United States on pages 4 and 5? Together, how do they help you understand the text?

Discuss the Chapter

➤ Which festivals will you visit in this book? Where did you find this information?

➤ What new information about harvests and the geography of different U.S. regions did you learn?

Have students begin filling in their **Harvest Festival Facts** charts with information from this chapter.

Comprehension Check Ask students the following questions. Encourage them to read aloud portions from the text that support their answers:

➤ What are some of the different foods that are harvested across America? (**recalling**)
➤ Why do different crops grow well in some regions but not in others? (**making inferences**)
➤ Why do people celebrate with harvest festivals? (**drawing conclusions**)

CELEBRATING STRAWBERRIES **PAGES 6–9**
Content Objective Students will learn about the annual strawberry festival in Oxnard, California, which celebrates one of the state's most important and profitable industries.

Discuss the Chapter
➤ Why do the people in California take the strawberry harvest so seriously?
➤ Which fact in this chapter did you find the most interesting? Explain your answer.
➤ Active readers look for the main ideas in the text and the details that support and tell more about the main ideas. What are the main ideas in this chapter? [1. More strawberries grow in California than in any other state. 2. California produces more than half of our country's fruit, vegetables, and nuts. 3. The people of Oxnard take strawberries seriously.]
➤ What supporting details tell more about the main ideas? [1. California's climate along the Pacific Coast is perfect for growing strawberries. They grow all year round. 2. Strawberries are one of California's biggest crops. Others include almonds, dates, kiwis, asparagus, and olives. 3. Farming is the area's top industry. Strawberries are the number one crop. Every year, about 90,000 people attend Oxnard's strawberry festival.]

> **Information Literacy: Reading a Chart**
> Look at the chart on page 7. Why do you think it is called a "pie chart"? Why did the writer choose to present facts in this type of chart?

Invite students to return to their **Harvest Festival Facts** charts to add information from this chapter.

Comprehension Check Have students respond in writing to the following prompts:

➤ In two or three sentences, describe the California Strawberry Festival. (**describing**)
➤ Explain why strawberries grow so well in California. (**explaining**)
➤ Florida is the second-largest strawberry-producing state. Use information from the map on page 4 to compare and contrast the climates and geographies of California and Florida. (**comparing and contrasting**)

HARVESTING POTATOES **PAGES 10–13**
Content Objective Reading about the Potato Days Festival in Barnesville, Minnesota, students will learn about the potato harvest and the importance of this crop to the Midwest economy.

Discuss the Chapter
➤ How has the potato festival changed since its early years? How is it the same?
➤ In what ways does the Potato Days Festival help bring people and communities together?
➤ How are the climate and soil conditions for potatoes different from those of strawberries?

 Information Literacy: Reading a Fact Box
Why is the information about eating potatoes set off in the Fact Box on page 11?

Have students add the information they learned in this chapter to their **Harvest Festival Facts** charts.

Comprehension Check Ask students the following questions. Encourage them to read aloud the portions from the text that support their answers:

➤ How are potatoes harvested? (**tracing**)
➤ What details in this chapter describe how proud the people in Barnesville, Minnesota, are of their potato industry? (**interpreting information**)
➤ What activities at the Potato Day Festival make it different from harvest festivals described in the previous chapters? (**contrasting**)

GROWING RICE **PAGES 14–17**
Content Objective Students will learn about the International Rice Festival—the oldest and biggest harvest festival in the Southeast region. They will also discover why the conditions in this region make it ideal for growing rice.

Vocabulary: Recognizing
Multiple-Meaning Words

Tell students that the word *combines* on page 17 has two meanings. Ask a volunteer to read aloud the sentence in which it appears: *Then they dump the rice plants into combines.* Help the student pronounce the word correctly, stressing the first syllable: COM-bines. Point out that this is different from the way the word is usually pronounced: com-BINES. Tell students that the familiar word is a verb that means "mixes." Here it is a noun. To help students figure out the definition, have them read the next sentence. Then, invite a volunteer to think aloud, demonstrating how he or she arrived at a definition.

Discuss the Chapter
➤ What foods and products made from rice have you eaten or used?
➤ How is rice an important part of the culture in the Southeast?
➤ How is rice harvested?

Draw a Flow Chart on the chalkboard or on chart paper. Title it "Harvesting Rice" and ask students to put the steps for harvesting rice in sequence.

Harvesting Rice
Step 1
Plants turn from green to yellow.
Step 2
Farmers drain the water from the fields.
Step 3
Machines pluck the plants from the mud.
Step 4
Plants are dumped into combines.
Step 5
Grains of rice are separated from the rest of the plant.

Have students add the information they learned in this chapter to their **Harvest Festival Facts** charts.

Comprehension Check Ask students the following questions. Encourage them to read aloud the portions from the text that support their answers:

➤ How does the climate make parts of the Southeast ideal for growing rice? (**recalling**)
➤ Why would you expect Louisiana to grow more rice than West Virginia? (**making inferences**)
➤ How are the climate and soil conditions for rice different from those of strawberries and potatoes? (**contrasting**)

FISHING FOR OYSTERS PAGES 18–21
Content Objective Students discover that the St. Mary's County Oyster Festival, in Maryland, celebrates an important crop for the Northeast region—oysters. Unlike the crops discussed in the book so far, this harvest comes from the sea.

Discuss the Chapter
➤ Why is the Oyster Festival important to the people of Maryland?
➤ How are fish like other crops? How are they different?
➤ How is the Oyster Festival similar to and different from the Rice Festival?

Draw a Venn Diagram on the chalkboard or on chart paper and distribute copies of the Venn Diagram on page 9 to each student to fill in. Write "Oyster Festival" above the left section. Write "Rice Festival" above the right. Ask students to provide details specific to each festival. In the overlapping area, have students record details that both festivals share. As students discuss similarities and differences, record their ideas on the diagram.

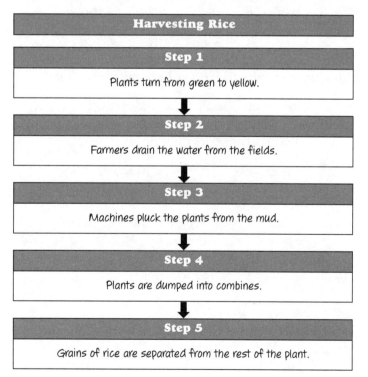

Reproducible page 9

Information Literacy: Reading a Diagram
Look at the diagram on page 21. What parts of the diagram can you see in the photograph on page 20? How does the diagram help you understand how oysters are harvested?

Invite students to share details they added to their **Harvest Festival Facts** charts from this chapter.

Comprehension Check Ask students the following questions. Encourage them to read aloud portions from the text that support their answers:

➤ What are oysters? How do people eat them? (describing)
➤ Why is Chesapeake Bay such a rich source of fish and shellfish? (explaining)
➤ How do you think a fisherman decides which oysters to keep from a haul? (evaluating; supporting an opinion)

THE HARVEST AND YOU PAGES 22–23
Content Objective Students will find out that there are harvest festivals for just about every kind of food that grows. They will also review the purpose of harvest, including providing food for us and income for farmers.

Discuss the Chapter
➤ Why do people hold festivals for almost every kind of food that grows?
➤ What needs do harvests fill?

Have students add the information from this chapter to their **Harvest Festival Facts** charts.

Comprehension Check Ask students the following questions. Encourage them to read aloud portions of the text that support their answers.

➤ How big is a chokecherry and how does it taste? (recalling)
➤ Why are farm and fishing harvests shipped to other states? (making inferences)
➤ In what way does this chapter summarize the book? (interpreting information)

After Reading
Ask students what they learned about harvest festivals. Then have students revisit their **Harvest Festival Facts** charts. Give them an opportunity to add to their charts and make sure they are complete. Collect the charts and keep them in students' assessment folders.

Responding to the Book: Personal Evaluation
Encourage students to share their personal responses to the book by asking the following questions:

➤ Which harvest festival in the book would you especially like to attend? Why?
➤ Is there anything you read about harvests that you did not understand? What can you do to understand it better?

Related Newbridge Books
Discovery Links
All About Potatoes
Fair Day USA
Festivals for All Seasons
Heartlands

Read to Learn
Apple Country
Corn: An American Invention
Fishing for a Living
Peanut Farming

Name: _____

Date: _____

Crop	Location	Festival Month	Climate/ Soil	Events	First Festival Year	
	Ohio					
Strawberries					1983	
				Potato sack fashion show		
			Warm, long growing season, lots of rain, flooded fields			Attracts about ten times the town's population
	Maryland					
Choke-cherries						

Copyright © Sundance/Newbridge Educational Publishing

Venn Diagram

Name: _____

Date: _____

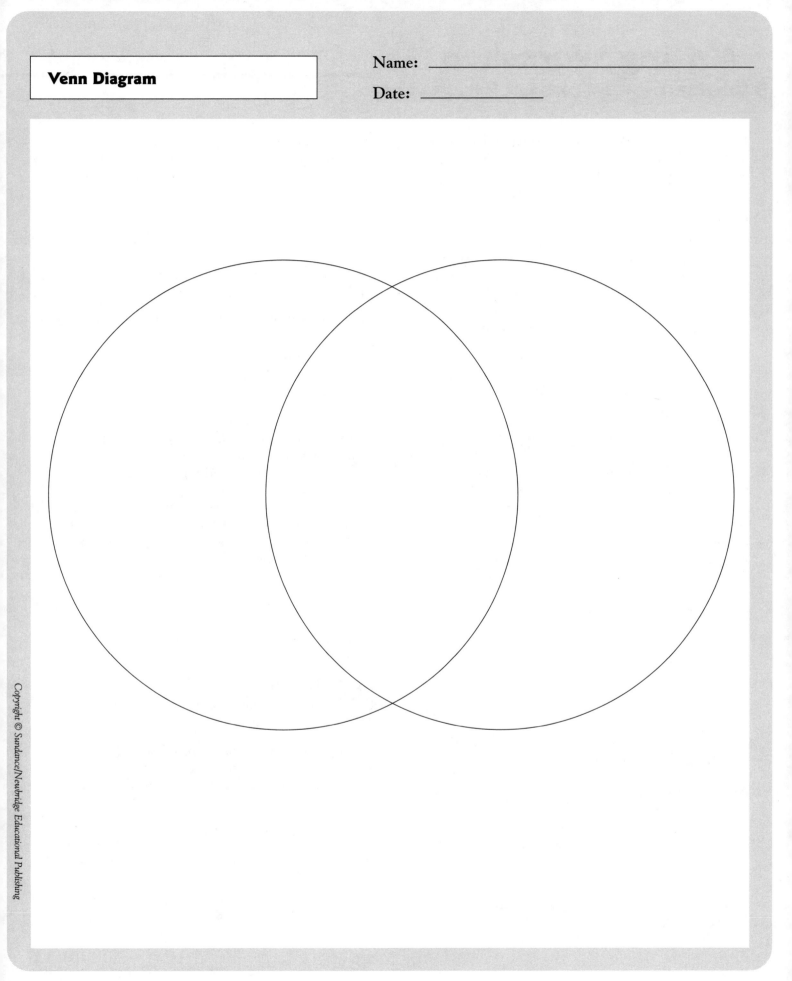

Writing Workshop
Compare-and-Contrast Paragraphs

In the Writing Workshop, students will use compare-and-contrast paragraphs they read in *Harvest Time* as models for writing. They will practice writing compare-and-contrast paragraphs of their own.

USING THE BOOK AS A MODEL

Invite students to open their books to page 20. Have a volunteer read aloud the first paragraph. Explore with the class what they learned from this paragraph. [the similarities and differences between the crops of the Northeast and the crops of other regions] Ask the following questions and record students' answers on a Venn Diagram on the chalkboard:

➤ How is the Northeast like other regions? [All have valuable farmland; all make money from fruits, vegetables, and grains.]
➤ What harvest does the Northeast have that the Midwest does not? [seafood]

Be sure students understand that *comparisons* are similarities, while *contrasts* are differences. Then have students identify words the writer uses to signal comparison and contrast. [The word *like* is used in the first sentence to show comparison. The word *however* is used in the third sentence to show contrast.] Arrange students in small groups to skim the rest of the chapter to find signal words for comparisons and contrasts.

➤ How do signal words help readers identify similarities and differences?
➤ What other words and phrases could you use to show similarities? [*similarly, likewise, as well, in the same way, too*]
➤ What other words and phrases could you use to show differences? [*but, yet, on the other hand, nevertheless, in contrast*]

Next, have students look at page 16 and ask a volunteer to read the first paragraph. Lead students to notice that this paragraph compares Louisiana with other states in the Southeast. Have them look for signal words here. [*not only, too*]

Guide the class to analyze the rest of the paragraphs on the page for comparisons and contrasts. Ask:

➤ How can you tell if the author did a good job comparing and contrasting two different things? [The similarities and differences are easy to identify.]
➤ Why do writers use special words to show comparisons and contrasts? [to help readers follow their logic]

Post a list of compare-and-contrast signal words for students to refer to when they begin writing.

WRITING A COMPARE-AND-CONTRAST PARAGRAPH

Invite students to write a compare-and-contrast paragraph of their own. Tell them that they can use the paragraphs they revisited as models.

Prewrite

Have students work in pairs to brainstorm a list of topics that would be suitable for a compare-and-contrast paragraph. To help students get started, suggest they think of something they know well, and then think of two examples of that item. (Examples: games or sports, cars, singers or actors, TV shows, movies.) Next, have each student choose a topic from the list. Suggest that students use a Venn Diagram (TG page 9) to compare and contrast their two items.

Draft

Direct students to write their compare-and-contrast paragraphs on their own. Remind them to use compare-and-contrast signal words to help make their comparisons clear.

Reminder:
Remind students of the key elements in a compare-and-contrast paragraph:

➤ Topics or items that can be compared
➤ Similarities and differences
➤ Compare-and-contrast signal words

Revise

Allow students time to revise their paragraphs.

➤ Have them check for compare-and-contrast signal words.
➤ Have them be sure the descriptions of similarities and differences are clear.

Target Skill: Signal Words

▶ Model the Target Skill

Display the overhead transparency on page 12 of this Guide. Ask students if they think this paragraph clearly compares and contrasts two types of fruit. Then have them rate the paragraph, using the following rubric:

3. I could understand the paragraph easily because it compares and contrasts information clearly.

2. I had some trouble understanding the paragraph because it does not compare and contrast all the information clearly.

1. I found the paragraph confusing because it does not clearly compare and contrast information.

Students should conclude that the paragraph is not clear because it lacks words that compare and contrast. Without signal words and phrases, it is difficult to understand how the two items are alike and different. If students have trouble making these observations on their own, help them by thinking aloud:

The first sentence mentions strawberries and apples, so I know that the paragraph will be about these two fruits. As I continue, I read facts about each fruit, but it's not clear how they are connected. If the writer used words that clearly compare and contrast strawberries and apples, then I would follow the paragraph more easily and understand how these two fruits are the same in some ways and different in others.

On the transparency, insert a caret between the words *are* and *fun* in the first sentence. Above it write *both*. Insert a caret in front of the third sentence and above it write *However*, and make *you* lowercase. Discuss with students why these revisions make the paragraph easier to follow and understand.

▶ Apply the Target Skill

Act as a scribe as the class works together to revise the rest of the paragraph. The revised paragraph should include signal words that make the comparisons and contrasts clear to the reader. Here is one possible result of the revision:

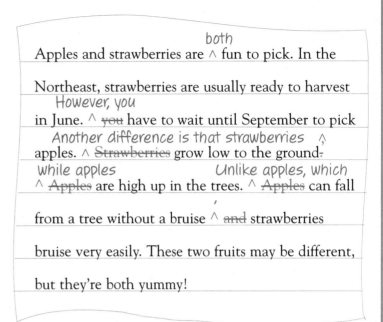

Once students are satisfied with their improvements, have them rate the revised paragraph, applying the same rubric they used before they revised. Ask volunteers to share their ratings and discuss their reasons.

▶ Practice the Target Skill

Encourage students to make their own paragraphs clearer and easier to follow by including compare-and-contrast signal words as needed.

Proofread and Publish

Have students read their paragraphs for correct spelling, punctuation, and capitalization. Then have students form small groups. Ask them to share revisions they have made and to discuss whether they think their revisions made their writing clearer and easier to understand.

Reflect on Your Work

Reproduce and distribute the Writer's Checklist on page 13 of this Guide and allow time for students to make their evaluations. Tell students that you will collect their paragraphs and checklists to add your ratings at a later time. You may wish to hold conferences with individual students to discuss how they can improve their writing in the future.

Writing Sample

Name: _____

Date: _____

Apples and strawberries are fun to pick. In the

Northeast, strawberries are usually ready to

harvest in June. You have to wait until September

to pick apples. Strawberries grow low to the

ground. Apples are high up in the trees. Apples

can fall from a tree without a bruise and

strawberries bruise very easily. These two fruits

may be different, but they're both yummy!

Writer's Checklist	Name: _____
	Date: _____

Rate your own writing. Think about your answer to each question in the "Question" column. Then give yourself a rating. Your teacher will give you a rating, too.

Yes, I did a great job = 3   Almost, but not quite = 1
Yes, but I could do better = 2   No, but I'll do this next time = 0

Question	Student Evaluation	Teacher Evaluation
Did I clearly state what I'm comparing and contrasting?		
Did I make at least one comparison?		
Did I use at least one comparison signal word or phrase?		
Did I make at least one contrast?		
Did I use at least one contrast signal word or phrase?		
Are my sentences in an order that makes sense?		

Newbridge Read to Learn: Social Studies

A. Select the answer that best completes each sentence. Write the letter of the answer on the line.

1. The region of the United States for which this book does not include a harvest festival is the _____.
   (a) Southwest   (c) Midwest
   (b) Northeast   (d) West

2. California produces many crops because the weather is mild, and _____.
   (a) many workers live along the West Coast   (c) the nights are wet and foggy
   (b) the growing season is 12 months long   (d) people across America buy many kinds of fruit

3. Potatoes grow best in soil that is _____.
   (a) hilly and moist   (c) level, rich, and moist
   (b) level, sandy, and dry   (d) hilly, sandy, and dry

4. The Southeast is a good place to grow rice because the climate is _____.
   (a) warm and dry   (c) warm and rainy
   (b) cool and dry   (d) cool and rainy

5. The Chokecherry Festival is held in _____.
   (a) Maine   (c) Maryland
   (b) Mississippi   (d) Montana

B. Answer the questions below with complete sentences. Write on the back of this page or on a separate sheet of paper.

1. Why are harvest festivals held at different times of the year?

2. Why is America able to produce such a large variety of crops?

3. Why do farmers poison the tops of the potato plants?

4. Why is rice considered part of the culture in the Southeast?

5. Why is Chesapeake Bay important for "fishing crops"?

Answers on inside front cover.

Performance Assessment	Name: _____
	Date: _____

A. Choose one of the regions described in this book. Fill in the chart with information about this region and its harvest(s).

Region: _____

Harvest Festival(s)	Climate	Land and Water

B. Imagine you are writing a travel brochure for people who are interested in attending a harvest festival in the region you chose in the chart above. Use the information in the chart to convince people to come to the harvest festival. In addition to your writing, draw pictures to make it more inviting.

Name: _____

Date: _____

Reflect on your work. Think about each statement in the first column. Then give yourself a rating:

Yes, I did a great job = 3   **Almost, but not quite = 1**

Yes, but I could do better = 2   **No, but I'll do this next time = 0**

For each rating of 0, 1, or 2 you gave yourself, go back and try to improve your work. Your teacher will rate your work after you have had a chance to make improvements.

Reflect on Your Work	Your Score	Your Teacher's Score
I chose a region in which there are one or more harvest festivals in the book.		
I listed the harvest festivals from that region.		
I described the region's climate.		
I listed features of the land and water in the region.		
I used the information in the chart to write a travel brochure for people interested in attending a harvest festival in the region.		